Published by: Red Cow Creative Content, LLC

Cover Design by: William Baughman

CIP Data on file

ISBN-10: 9798598860120

HOPE IS BACK

The Inaugural Day Speeches of
Joe Biden & Kamala Harris

Published by
Red Cow Creative Content

HOPE IS BACK

THE INAUGURAL DAY SPEECHES OF
JOE BIDEN & KAMALA HARRIS

CHAPTER ONE

Joseph Robinette Biden Jr.

Presidential Oath of Office

I Joseph Robinette Biden Jr. do solemnly swear that I will faithfully execute the Office of President of the United States, and will to the best of my ability, preserve, protect and defend the Constitution of the United States. So help me God.

Inauguration Address

Delivered January 20, 2021 at 11:48 a.m. on the capital steps in front of three former Presidents, William Clinton. George W. Bush, and Barack Obama; two former Vice Presidents, Dan Quayle and Mike Pence; one sitting Vice President, Kamala Harris; and every member of the Supreme Court.

Chief Justice Roberts, Vice President Harris, Speaker Pelosi, Leader Schumer, Leader McConnell, Vice President Pence, distinguished guests, and my fellow Americans.

This is America's day.

This is democracy's day.

A day of history and hope.

Of renewal and resolve.

Through a crucible for the ages America has been tested anew and America has risen to the challenge.

Today, we celebrate the triumph not of a candidate, but of a cause, the cause of democracy.

The will of the people has been heard and the will of the people has been heeded.

We have learned again that democracy is precious.

Democracy is fragile.

And at this hour, my friends, democracy has prevailed.

So now, on this hallowed ground where just days ago violence sought to shake this Capitol's very foundation, we come together as one nation, under God, indivisible, to carry out the peaceful transfer of power as we have for more than two centuries.

We look ahead in our uniquely American way – restless, bold, optimistic – and set our sights on the nation we know we can be and we must be.

I thank my predecessors of both parties for their presence here.

I thank them from the bottom of my heart.

You know the resilience of our Constitution and the strength of our nation.

As does President Carter, who I spoke to last night but who cannot be with us today, but whom we salute for his lifetime of service.

I have just taken the sacred oath each of these patriots took — an oath first sworn by George Washington.

But the American story depends not on any one of us, not on some of us, but on all of us.

On "We the People" who seek a more perfect Union.

This is a great nation and we are a good people.

Over the centuries through storm and strife, in peace and in war, we have come so far. But we still have far to go.

We will press forward with speed and urgency, for we have much to do in this winter of peril and possibility.

Much to repair.

Much to restore.

Much to heal.

Much to build.

And much to gain.

Few periods in our nation's history have been more challenging or difficult than the one we're in now.

A once-in-a-century virus silently stalks the country.

It's taken as many lives in one year as America lost in all of World War II.

Millions of jobs have been lost.

Hundreds of thousands of businesses closed.

A cry for racial justice some 400 years in the making moves us. The dream of justice for all will be deferred no longer.

A cry for survival comes from the planet itself. A cry that can't be any more desperate or any more clear.

And now, a rise in political extremism, white supremacy, domestic terrorism that we must confront and we will defeat.

14

To overcome these challenges – to restore the soul and to secure the future of America – requires more than words.

It requires that most elusive of things in a democracy:

Unity.

Unity.

In another January in Washington, on New Year's Day 1863, Abraham Lincoln signed the Emancipation Proclamation.

When he put pen to paper, the President said, "If my name ever goes down into history it will be for this act and my whole soul is in it."

My whole soul is in it.

Today, on this January day, my whole soul is in this:

Bringing America together.

Uniting our people.

And uniting our nation.

I ask every American to join me in this cause.

Uniting to fight the common foes we face:

Anger, resentment, hatred.

Extremism, lawlessness, violence.

Disease, joblessness, hopelessness.

With unity we can do great things. Important things.

We can right wrongs.

We can put people to work in good jobs.

We can teach our children in safe schools.

We can overcome this deadly virus.

We can reward work, rebuild the middle class, and make health care

secure for all.

We can deliver racial justice.

We can make America, once again, the leading force for good in the world.

I know speaking of unity can sound to some like a foolish fantasy.

I know the forces that divide us are deep and they are real.

But I also know they are not new.

Our history has been a constant struggle between the American ideal that we are all created equal and the harsh, ugly reality that racism, nativism, fear, and demonization have long torn us apart.

The battle is perennial.

Victory is never assured.

Through the Civil War, the Great Depression, World War, 9/11, through struggle, sacrifice, and setbacks, our "better angels" have always prevailed.

In each of these moments, enough of us came together to carry all of us forward.

And, we can do so now.

History, faith, and reason show the way, the way of unity.

We can see each other not as adversaries but as neighbors.

We can treat each other with dignity and respect.

We can join forces, stop the shouting, and lower the temperature.

For without unity, there is no peace, only bitterness and fury.

No progress, only exhausting outrage.

No nation, only a state of chaos.

This is our historic moment of crisis and challenge, and unity is the path forward.

And, we must meet this moment as the United States of America.

If we do that, I guarantee you, we will not fail.

We have never, ever, ever failed in America when we have acted together.

And so today, at this time and in this place, let us start afresh.

All of us.

Let us listen to one another.

Hear one another.

See one another.

Show respect to one another.

Politics need not be a raging fire destroying everything in its path.

Every disagreement doesn't have to be a cause for total war.

And, we must reject a culture in which facts themselves are manipulated and even manufactured.

My fellow Americans, we have to be different than this.

America has to be better than this.

And, I believe America is better than this.

Just look around.

Here we stand, in the shadow of a Capitol dome that was completed amid the Civil War, when the Union itself hung in the balance.

Yet we endured and we prevailed.

Here we stand looking out to the great Mall where Dr. King spoke of his dream.

Here we stand, where 108 years ago at another inaugural, thousands of protestors tried to block brave women from marching for the right to vote.

Today, we mark the swearing-in of the first woman in American history elected to national office – Vice President Kamala Harris.

Don't tell me things can't change.

Here we stand across the Potomac from Arlington National Cemetery, where heroes who gave the last full measure of devotion rest in eternal peace.

And here we stand, just days after a riotous mob thought they could use violence to silence the will of the people, to stop the work of our democracy, and to drive us from this sacred ground.

That did not happen.

It will never happen.

Not today.

Not tomorrow.

Not ever.

To all those who supported our campaign I am humbled by the faith you have placed in us.

To all those who did not support us, let me say this: Hear me out as we move forward. Take a measure of me and my heart.

And if you still disagree, so be it.

That's democracy. That's America. The right to dissent peaceably, within the guardrails of our Republic, is perhaps our nation's greatest strength.

Yet hear me clearly: Disagreement must not lead to disunion.

And I pledge this to you: I will be a President for all Americans.

I will fight as hard for those who did not support me as for those who did.

Many centuries ago, Saint Augustine, a saint of my church, wrote that a people was a multitude defined by the common objects of their love.

What are the common objects we love that define us as Americans?

I think I know.

Opportunity.

Security.

Liberty.

Dignity.

Respect.

Honor.

And, yes, the truth.

Recent weeks and months have taught us a painful lesson.

There is truth and there are lies.

Lies told for power and for profit.

And each of us has a duty and responsibility, as citizens, as Americans, and especially as leaders – leaders who have pledged to honor our Constitution and protect our nation — to defend the truth and to defeat the lies.

I understand that many Americans view the future with some fear and trepidation.

I understand they worry about their jobs, about taking care of their families, about what comes next.

I get it.

But the answer is not to turn inward, to retreat into competing factions, distrusting those who don't look like you do, or worship the way you do, or don't get their news from the same sources you do.

We must end this uncivil war that pits red against blue, rural versus urban, conservative versus liberal.

We can do this if we open our souls instead of hardening our hearts.

If we show a little tolerance and humility.

If we're willing to stand in the other person's shoes just for a moment.

Because here is the thing about life: There is no accounting for what fate will deal you.

There are some days when we need a hand.

There are other days when we're called on to lend one.

That is how we must be with one another.

And, if we are this way, our country will be stronger, more prosperous, more ready for the future.

My fellow Americans, in the work ahead of us, we will need each other.

We will need all our strength to persevere through this dark winter.

We are entering what may well be the toughest and deadliest period of the virus.

We must set aside the politics and finally face this pandemic as one nation.

I promise you this: as the Bible says weeping may endure for a night but joy cometh in the morning.

We will get through this, together

The world is watching today.

So here is my message to those beyond our borders: America has been tested and we have come out stronger for it.

We will repair our alliances and engage with the world once again.

Not to meet yesterday's challenges, but today's and tomorrow's.

We will lead not merely by the example of our power but by the power of our example.

We will be a strong and trusted partner for peace, progress, and security.

We have been through so much in this nation.

And, in my first act as President, I would like to ask you to join me in a moment of silent prayer to remember all those we lost this past year to the pandemic.

To those 400,000 fellow Americans – mothers and fathers, husbands and wives, sons and daughters, friends, neighbors, and co-workers.

We will honor them by becoming the people and nation we know we can and should be.

Let us say a silent prayer for those who lost their lives, for those they left behind, and for our country.

Amen.

This is a time of testing.

We face an attack on democracy and on truth.

A raging virus.

Growing inequity.

The sting of systemic racism.

A climate in crisis.

America's role in the world.

Any one of these would be enough to challenge us in profound ways.

But the fact is we face them all at once, presenting this nation with the gravest of responsibilities.

Now we must step up.

All of us.

It is a time for boldness, for there is so much to do.

And, this is certain.

We will be judged, you and I, for how we resolve the cascading crises of our era.

Will we rise to the occasion?

Will we master this rare and difficult hour?

Will we meet our obligations and pass along a new and better world for our children?

I believe we must and I believe we will.

And when we do, we will write the next chapter in the American story.

It's a story that might sound something like a song that means a lot to me.

It's called "American Anthem" and there is one verse stands out for me:

"The work and prayers

of centuries have brought us to this day

What shall be our legacy?

What will our children say?…

Let me know in my heart

When my days are through

America

America

I gave my best to you."

Let us add our own work and prayers to the unfolding story of our nation.

If we do this then when our days are through our children and our children's children will say of us they gave their best.

They did their duty.

They healed a broken land.

My fellow Americans, I close today where I began, with a sacred oath.

Before God and all of you I give you my word.

I will always level with you.

I will defend the Constitution.

I will defend our democracy.

I will defend America.

I will give my all in your service thinking not of power, but of possibilities.

Not of personal interest, but of the public good.

And together, we shall write an American story of hope, not fear.

Of unity, not division.

Of light, not darkness.

An American story of decency and dignity.

Of love and of healing.

Of greatness and of goodness.

May this be the story that guides us.

The story that inspires us.

The story that tells ages yet to come that we answered the call of history.

We met the moment.

That democracy and hope, truth and justice, did not die on our watch but thrived.

That our America secured liberty at home and stood once again as a beacon to the world.

That is what we owe our forebearers, one another, and generations to follow.

So, with purpose and resolve we turn to the tasks of our time.

Sustained by faith.

Driven by conviction.

And, devoted to one another and to this country we love with all our hearts.

May God bless America and may God protect our troops.

Thank you, America.

CHAPTER TWO

Kamala Devi Harris

Vice Presidential Oath of Office

I, Kamala Devi Harris, do solemnly swear that I will support and defend the Constitution of the United States against all enemies, foreign and domestic; that I will bear true faith and allegiance to the same; that I take this obligation freely, without any mental reservation or purpose of evasion; that I will well and faithfully discharge the duties of the office upon which I am about to enter. So help me God.

Remarks by Vice President Kamala Harris at the Celebration of America

Good evening. It is my honor to be here.

To stand on the shoulders of those who came before.

To speak tonight as your Vice President.

In many ways, this moment embodies our character as a nation.

It demonstrates who we are.

Even in dark times —

We not only dream. We do.

We not only see what has been, we see what can be.

We shoot for the moon, and then we plant our flag on it.

We are bold, fearless, and ambitious.

We are undaunted in our belief that we shall overcome, that we will rise up.

This is American Aspiration.

In the middle of the Civil War, Abraham Lincoln saw a better future and built it — with land-grant colleges and the transcontinental railroad.

In the middle of the civil rights movement, Dr. King fought for racial justice and economic justice.

American Aspiration is what drove the women of this nation, throughout history, to demand equal rights.

And the authors of the Bill of Rights to claim freedoms that had rarely been written down before.

A Great Experiment takes great determination — the will to do the work and then the wisdom to keep refining, keep tinkering, keep perfecting.

The same determination is being realized in America today.

I see it in the scientists who are transforming the future.

I see it in the parents who are nurturing generations to come.

In the innovators and the educators.

In everyone, everywhere who is building a better life for themselves, their families, and their communities.

This, too, is American Aspiration.

This is what President Joe Biden has called upon us to summon now.

The courage to see beyond crisis.

To do what is hard.

To do what is good.

To unite.

To believe in ourselves.

Believe in our country.

Believe in what we can do—together.

Thank you. And may God bless America.

CHAPTER THREE

Inauguration Day Poem

"The Hill We Climb"
By
Amanda Gorman

When day comes we ask ourselves

Where can we find light in this never-ending shade?

The loss we carry,

A sea we must wade.

We braved the belly of the beast;

We've learned that quiet isn't always peace.

And the norms and notions of what just is

Isn't always justice.

And yet the dawn is ours before we knew it.

Somehow we do it;

Somehow we've weathered and witnessed

A nation that isn't broken but simply unfinished.

We, the successors of a country and a time

Where a skinny black girl descended from slaves

And raised by a single mother can dream of becoming president,

Only to find herself reciting for one.

And yes we are far from polished, far from pristine,

But that doesn't mean we aren't striving to form a union that is perfect.

We are striving to forge a union with purpose,

To compose a country committed to all cultures, colors, characters and conditions of man.

And so we lift our gaze not to what stands between us,

But what stands before us.

We close the divide, because we know to put our future first,

We must first put our differences aside.

We lay down our arms

So we can reach out our arms to one another.

We seek harm to none and harmony for all.

Let the globe, if nothing else, say this is true:

That even as we grieved, we grew,

That even as we hurt, we hoped,

That even as we tired, we tried,

That we'll forever be tied together, victorious—

Not because we will never again know defeat

But because we will never again sow division.

Scripture tells us to envision

That everyone shall sit under their own vine and fig tree,

And no one shall make them afraid.

If we're to live up to our own time,

then victory won't lie in the blade but in all the bridges
we've made.

That is the promised glade,

The hill we climb if only we dare it.

Because being American is more than a pride we inherit,

It's the past we step into and how we repair it.

We've seen a force that would shatter our nation rather than share it,

Would destroy our country if it meant delaying democracy.

And this effort very nearly succeeded,

But while democracy can be periodically delayed

It can never be permanently defeated.

In this truth, in this faith we trust,

For while we have our eyes on the future, history has its eyes on us.

This is the era of just redemption.

We feared at its inception.

We did not feel prepared to be the heirs of such a terrifying hour,

But within it we found the power

To author a new chapter,

To offer hope and laughter,

To ourselves sow. While once we asked:

How could we possibly prevail over catastrophe?

Now we assert: How could catastrophe possibly prevail over us?

We will not march back to what was,

But move to what shall be,

A country that is bruised but whole,

Benevolent but bold,

Fierce and free.

We will not be turned around or interrupted by intimidation

Because we know our inaction and inertia will be the inheritance of the next generation.

Our blunders become their burdens

But one thing is certain:

If we merge mercy with might and might with right,

Then love becomes our legacy

And change our children's birthright.

So let us leave behind a country better than the one we were left.

With every breath of my bronze pounded chest,

We will raise this wounded world into a wondrous one.

We will rise from the golden hills of the West.

We will rise from the windswept Northeast where our forefathers first realized revolution.

We will rise from the lakeland cities of the Midwestern states.

We will rise from the sunbaked South.

We will rebuild, reconcile and recover

In every known nook of our nation,

In every corner called our country,

Our people, diverse and beautiful,

Will emerge battered and beautiful.

When day comes we step out of the shade,

Aflame and unafraid.

The new dawn blooms as we free it.

For there is always light if only we're brave enough to see it,

If only we're brave enough to be it.

Thank you for purchasing "Hope is Back." A portion of all proceeds will go towards ending food insecurity in the United States.

Primary content for "Hope Is Back"
courrtesy of the White House Press Office.